Garfield eats his heart out

BY: JIM DAVIS

BALLANTINE BOOKS · NEW YORK

All rights reserved under International and Pan-American Copyright Conventions. Published in the United States by Ballantine Books, a division of Random House, Inc., New York, and simultaneously in Canada by Random House of Canada Limited, Toronto, Canada.

Library of Congress Catalog Card Number: 82-90830
ISBN: 0-345-30912-X

Manufactured in the United States of America

First Edition: March 1983

10 9 8 7 6 5 4 3 2 1

GARFIELD DIET TIPS

1. Never go back for seconds—get it all the first time.

2. Set your scales back five pounds.

3. Never accept a candygram.

4. Don't date Sara Lee.

5. Vegetables are a must on a diet. I suggest carrot cake, zucchini bread and pumpkin pie.

6. Never start a diet cold turkey (maybe cold roast beef, cold lasagna...).

7. Try to cut back. Leave the cherry off your ice cream sundae.

8. Hang around people fatter than you.

BURP

GARFIELD

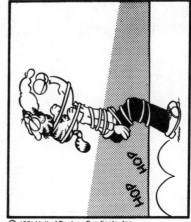

I'M GETTING OUT OF THIS TREE
JIM DAVIS
7-8
BOING!
I DIDN'T ALLOW FOR MY RESILIENT NATURE
© 1981 United Feature Syndicate, Inc.

POOR ME... STUCK UP A TREE
JIM DAVIS
7-9
THINGS COULD BE WORSE, I GUESS
© 1981 United Feature Syndicate, Inc.

HERE IT COMES, FOLKS

LASAGNA ANYONE?

I'LL PASS

NOPE

I'M ON A DIET

I THINK I'LL WAIT FOR DESSERT

I JUST ATE

TAH-DAH!

JIM DAVIS 8-9

© 1981 United Feature Syndicate, Inc.

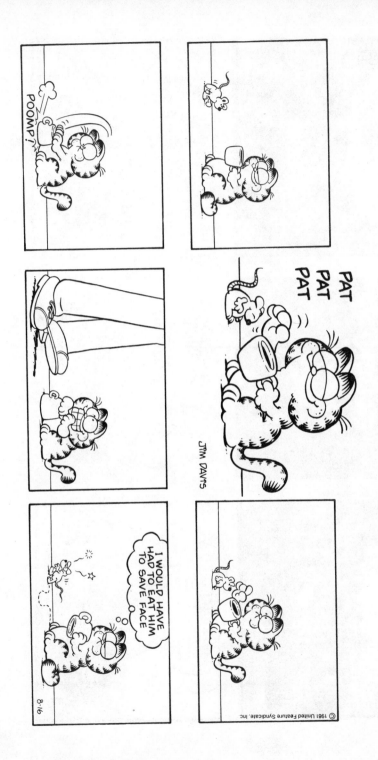

AND HIS SIDEKICK, LAWRENCE OF BOXER SHORTS

EVEN AFTER SHAVE LOTION TASTES GOOD IF YOU'RE DRY ENOUGH

JIM DAVIS 8-17

HERE COMES DON JUAN

JIM DAVIS

CLUCK CLUCK CLUCK

LOOK OUT, SUNNY BEACHES

8-18

STOWING AWAY IN JON'S SUITCASE IS THIRSTY WORK

THIS IS THE LIFE, GARFIELD

8-21

YOU KNOW YOU'RE ON VACATION WHEN YOU SEE WOMEN IN BIKINIS, HIBISCUS BLOSSOMS IN THE POOL...

AND LA CUCARACHAS IN THE SOCK DRAWER

JIM DAVIS

PARDON ME... I BELIEVE I DROPPED MY NOBEL PEACE PRIZE AROUND HERE SOMEWHERE

BEAT IT, CREEP

JIM DAVIS

8-22

HA HA HA!

WHAT A GREAT PLOT, FINE ACTING, SUPER PHOTOGRAPHY

I LOVE COMMERCIALS

JIM DAVIS

YOU'RE NO LONGER A KITTEN, GARFIELD

HOW CAN YOU HOGS STAND TO LIE IN A WALLER ALL DAY?

THE MUD KEEPS THE FLIES OFF AND KEEPS US COOL

AND IF WE EVER GET OUT, THE MUD DRYS INSTANTLY

JIM DAVIS

9-25

IT'S TIME TO GO HOME, GARFIELD. LET ME KNOCK THAT MUD OFF YOU

CRACK!

THANKS... I THINK

JIM DAVIS

9-26

JIM DAVIS
10-21

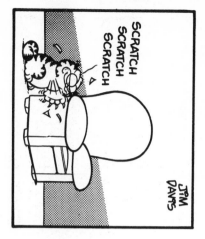

© 1981 United Feature Syndicate, Inc.

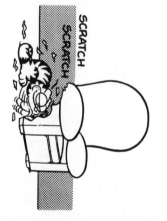

© 1981 United Feature Syndicate, Inc.

LOOK, GARFIELD. MOM MADE A SWEATER FOR YOU

I'VE NEVER LIKED YOUR MOTHER

JIM DAVIS 11-9

JIM DAVIS 11-10

© 1981 United Feature Syndicate, Inc.

11-22 © 1981 United Feature Syndicate, Inc.

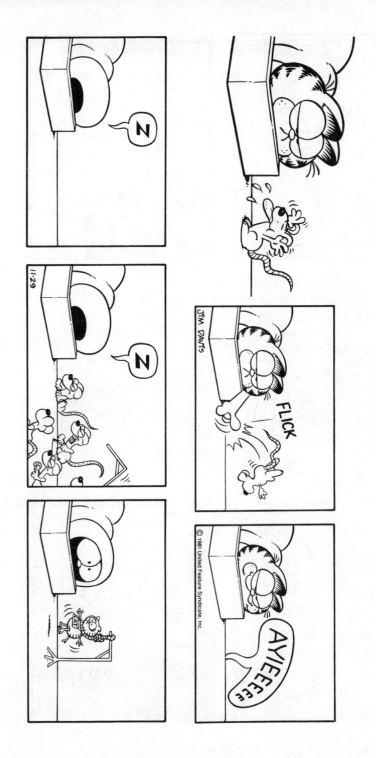

WHAT ARE YOU DOING BACK IN BED, GARFIELD? IT'S NOT EVEN NOON YET

AS FAR AS I'M CONCERNED, THE DAY IS OVER

JtM DAVtS

12-6

© 1981 United Feature Syndicate, Inc.

12-25

WHAT WOULD YOU LIKE FOR CHRISTMAS, GARFIELD?

WORLD PEACE

JIM DAVIS

12-24

AND HERE'S SOMETHING FOR JOLLY OLD SAINT NICK

JIM DAVIS

© 1981 United Feature Syndicate, Inc.

SERIOUSLY THOUGH

HOW ABOUT ANOTHER BUTTON FOR POOKY HERE?

© 1981 United Feature Syndicate, Inc.

HO HO HO

Garfield Goes Globetrotting

The GARFIELD strip appears worldwide.

Here's GARFIELD in English...

Spanish...

French...

Danish...

German...